GENETIC DISORDERS

BY ROBIN DOAK

Table of Contents

Introduction

A man has eleven toes. A boy has webbed feet. A woman grows a beard. Each of those things happens because of a **genetic disorder** (jeh-NEH-tik dis-OR-der). A genetic disorder occurs when a person's **genes** aren't working properly. Genes contain instructions that tell the cells in your body how to grow and develop. If a person's genes are defective, damaged, or missing, a genetic disorder can result. A person with six fingers on one hand has a genetic disorder.

There are many types of genetic disorders. Some disorders are passed down from parent to child. Others happen when chemicals or environmental factors affect genes.

Genetic disorders can affect different parts of the body. Scientists are trying to figure out what causes genetic disorders. They have learned that genes are made up of DNA. DNA is a complex substance that stores and transmits a cell's genetic information.

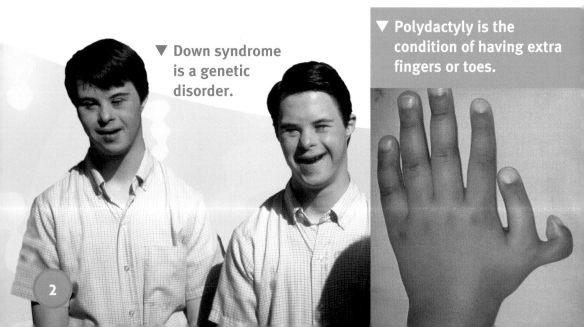

▼ Down syndrome is a genetic disorder.

▼ Polydactyly is the condition of having extra fingers or toes.

By studying DNA and genetic disorders, scientists figured out many of the causes of genetic disorders. They have learned how genetic disorders affect the body.

Today scientists try to find better ways to treat and prevent many conditions.

These include **genetic testing**, **gene therapy**, and **genetic engineering**.

Why is it important to study genetic disorders? How can these types of conditions affect people you know? Read on to find out. You will learn how your genes help shape who you are.

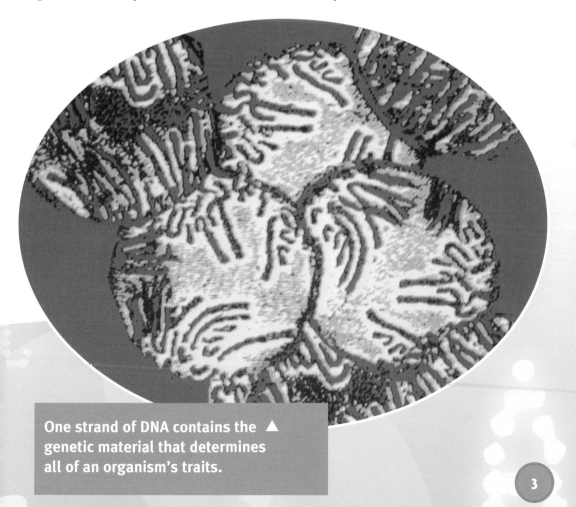

One strand of DNA contains the ▲ genetic material that determines all of an organism's traits.

Understanding Genetic Disorders

Scientists have identified more than 4,000 types of genetic disorders. Such disorders may arise when a person has extra copies of a gene or an extra DNA code disrupts the normal function of a gene. Some disorders are the result of **mutation** (myoo-TAY-shun). A mutation is a change in one or more genes. Mutations might cause parts of a gene to be missing. Sometimes mutations switch parts of the DNA code around. Each of those things may cause a disorder.

It's a Fact

Did you know that you have a lot in common with a fruit fly? Humans share the same genes as many animals, including these tiny insects that feed on fruit.

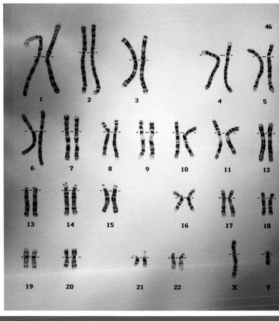

▲ **Chromosomes** (KROH-muh-somez) are sequences of DNA that include many genes.

About five percent of babies are born with a genetic disorder. To understand why, you need to understand **heredity** (huh-REH-dih-tee). Heredity is the passing of genes from parents to child. Each parent passes down half of his or her genes to the child. The genes control traits and many other things.

Sometimes parents pass a mutant gene to their child. Let's say one parent has a defective gene. There is a fifty percent chance that the child will receive a copy of that gene. Scientists think that every human carries between five to ten mutated genes. Just one mutated gene can cause health problems.

From Parents to Children

Genetic disorders can be passed from parent to child in several different ways. The illustration shows how an affected father can pass on a mutated gene. "Affected" means a person carries a faulty gene.

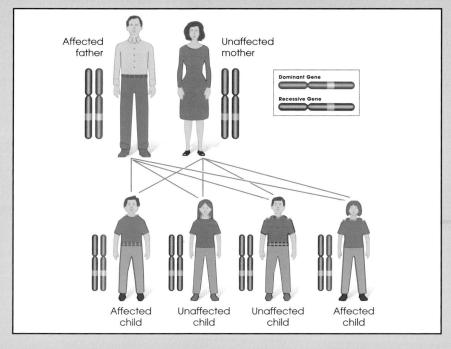

Affected father

Unaffected mother

Dominant Gene

Recessive Gene

Affected child

Unaffected child

Unaffected child

Affected child

Genetic disorders are common and can be harmless. About one out of every ten adults has a genetic defect. For example, people with polydactyly (pah-lee-DAK-tuh-lee) are born with extra fingers or toes. Such a condition usually has no effect on a person's quality of life. Those born with color-blindness can't tell the difference between certain colors.

Other genetic disorders are more serious. One such disease is neurofibromatosis (nuhr-oh-fy-broh-muh-TOH-suhs). It causes the body to develop in abnormal ways. Joseph Merrick likely had this disease as well as Proteus (PROH-tee-uhs) syndrome, another genetic disorder. His life was made into a movie called *The Elephant Man*. Merrick's skull and nose were very deformed. Some people said he looked like an elephant.

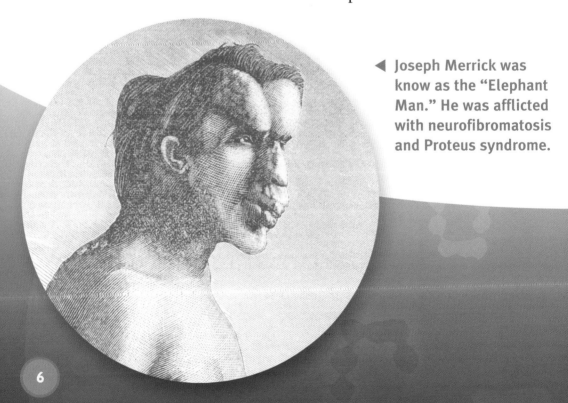

◀ Joseph Merrick was know as the "Elephant Man." He was afflicted with neurofibromatosis and Proteus syndrome.

Some genetic disorders may not show up right away. Instead, they cause problems as a person ages. Certain types of Alzheimer's disease usually appear when a person is sixty-five or older. Alzheimer's attacks parts of the brain. Thought, memory, and language abilities suffer. The disease makes it hard for people to do daily tasks and to remember things.

Some genetic defects can cause death. In fact, genetic disorders are one of the chief causes of infant deaths. Some babies are born without body parts. Others may be twins who fused together in the womb. Some twins are joined at the head, hips, or shoulders. Conjoined twins often share some body parts. About seventy-five percent of them don't survive. Some conjoined twins can live long lives while still attached to each other. Other conjoined twins are not so lucky. If doctors cannot separate them, they might not survive.

▲ Conjoined twins can sometimes be separated surgically, but many die as a result of their condition.

They Made a Difference

In 1905, English biologist William Bateson became the first person to use the word "genetics." He used it to describe a brand-new branch of biology. This branch studied heredity. It looked at the physical variations, or differences, in humans, animals, and plants. In the 1890s, Bateson performed experiments with chickens and peas. He proved that certain traits were passed from parent to offspring.

Learning More About Genetic Disorders

In the past, people didn't know that defective genes caused genetic disorders. Many people thought genetic disorders came from curses. Some thought that diseases were punishments. Others thought that if a pregnant woman saw certain things, her child would be born with a disease. As a result, people with genetic disorders were often treated poorly.

In the early 1900s, scientists began to understand heredity. They learned how physical traits are passed from parent to child. Scientists also began to learn more about medical conditions that can be passed down from parents. One such disease is cancer. Some people inherit genes from their parents that make them more likely to develop cancer.

Eleven-year-old Perri is a sixth grader. Since she was three years old, Perri has been living with diabetes. Diabetes is a disease that affects the body's ability to properly use glucose—a type of sugar.

How does diabetes affect your life each day?
I wear an insulin pump. It's a little machine that looks like a pager. It gives me injections of insulin that help keep me healthy. Before I eat, I have to test my blood sugar. I also have to be careful about what I eat.

Are there things you cannot do because of diabetes?
No, not really. It is hard to sleep over at a friend's house, though, because I always have to check my blood sugar.

Do any of your relatives have diabetes?
My dad has had diabetes since he was thirteen.

What would you like other kids to know about having diabetes?
Diabetes is hard to deal with, but as long as you take care of yourself, you can do anything you want to do.

Perhaps you inherited a gene that makes cancer more likely. This doesn't mean that cancer will develop. Something from the environment often needs to act on a person's genes first. Scientists also know that a person's environment plays a role in illness. Someone living in a windy desert might breathe dust. This can cause lung problems.

A person's habits can also increase the chances of becoming sick. For example, a person who is at risk of developing heart disease shouldn't smoke. Smoking increases the chances of becoming ill.

☑ POINT

Picture It

Draw a picture of yourself choosing healthy habits. Then write a caption explaining how your choices give you a better chance of avoiding problems in the future.

▲ The environment can interact with genetic conditions to cause some diseases.

Scientists use **gene mapping** to learn more about genetic disorders. Gene mapping is the process of locating a specific gene on a chromosome. A chromosome is a threadlike structure in a cell that carries all the genetic information passed on from one generation to the next. Humans have forty-six chromosomes arranged in twenty-three pairs. Genes come in pairs, too. There is one gene on each chromosome.

▲ genome research

They Made a Difference

In 1990, scientists began working on the Human Genome Project. A genome is all of the DNA in a living thing. The project's goal was to completely map human DNA. The scientists also wanted to identify the genes in the human body.

In 2003, scientists finished the project. Their findings concluded:

- 99.9 percent of all genetic material is the same in all humans.

- The function of 50 percent of all discovered genes is unknown.

- Humans have from 20,000 to 25,000 genes. This is much less than first thought.

Scientists continue to look for the exact location of each gene on the chromosomes. Such knowledge will allow doctors to better treat patients with genetic disorders. More research may help scientists prevent certain genetic disorders.

everyday science

Learn more about your own genes. Explore your family's past by creating a family tree. Look at the illustration below. Then start your own chart. Interview your parents and grandparents for any information you might need.

you

Common Genetic Disorders

Abnormal Chromosome Disorders

Abnormal chromosomes cause some types of genetic disorders. These types of disorders are common. They affect one out of every 200 infants. They are usually very serious. Many result in the death of the **fetus** (FEE-tus) before birth.

About one out of every 800 children is born with Down syndrome. People with Down syndrome usually have an extra copy of chromosome twenty-one. Scientists don't know how the extra copy causes the condition.

Children with Down syndrome usually look similar. They have small noses and large lips. They suffer from below-average mental development. Heart defects are among their other health problems.

◄ Spina bifida is thought to be caused by an interaction between multiple genes and the environment.

Another common chromosome disorder is Turner syndrome. This only affects females. About one out of every 2,500 girls is born with Turner syndrome. It's caused when part or all of an X chromosome is missing. The X chromosome helps determine the sex of a person. Females normally have two X chromosomes. Males have an X chromosome and a Y chromosome.

Women with Turner syndrome usually are short. They can't have children. They may also have other problems. These include a webbed neck, soft nails, or loss of hearing.

Chris Burke ▶

They Made a Difference

Down syndrome is a serious genetic disorder. But many people with this disorder live happy lives. One such person is Chris Burke. Burke was born in New York in 1965. He became interested in acting. In 1989, he won a role on the TV series *Life Goes On*.

In 1992, Burke wrote *A Special Kind of Hero*. This is an autobiography about living with Down syndrome. Today, Burke serves as a spokesperson for the National Down Syndrome Society. He tells people that it's a person's abilities not disabilities that matter.

Mutated Gene Disorders

There are thousands of genes that may mutate. Each mutated gene causes a different genetic disorder. Some disorders are caused by a single mutated gene. One such disorder is the most common type of dwarfism. Most people with this condition only grow to be 5 feet (1.5 meters) tall.

Marfan syndrome is caused by a single mutated gene on chromosome fifteen. This genetic disorder affects the body's connective tissues. The connective tissue isn't as stiff as it should be. It doesn't provide as much support as certain parts of the body need. People with Marfan syndrome develop arms, legs, and fingers that are unusually long and thin. They may also have other health conditions. These include vision problems and a deformed chest and heart.

▲ Dwarfism is one of the oldest recorded birth defects.

Historical Perspective

Picture Abraham Lincoln. He's very tall and thin. But do you think he had Marfan syndrome? In the 1960s, two doctors said that he did. They used historic documents and pictures as proof. Like people with Marfan syndrome, Lincoln had long limbs, an abnormal chest, and loose joints. Other medical experts disagreed. Lincoln lived longer than others with the disease did at the time. He also didn't have other symptoms of Marfan syndrome. For now, the mystery remains unsolved.

Another mutated gene causes hemophilia. Hemophilia affects the blood's ability to clot normally. People with hemophilia can bleed to death from small cuts.

Only mothers can pass on the mutated gene that causes hemophilia. That's because the gene is located on the X chromosome. However, the disorder almost always affects males. This happens because females, unlike males, have two copies of the X chromosome. So if one is faulty, the other one takes over. The healthy gene prevents the harmful effect.

It's a Fact

Queen Victoria passed the mutated gene for hemophilia to her children. Her daughters were carriers of the mutated gene. They married members of other ruling families. Soon, the disease spread to the royal families of Russia, Spain, and Germany. It became known as the Royal Disease.

◄ Tsarina Alexandra of Russia (granddaughter of Queen Victoria) was a carrier of hemophilia. Her son Alexei was afflicted with the disease.

Sickle Cell Anemia

Some types of genetic disorders mainly affect certain groups of people. One of these disorders is sickle cell anemia. About one in every 500 African Americans suffers from this disorder.

Sickle cell anemia is passed from parent to child. It causes hard, sticky, sickle-shaped blood cells. Sickle means shaped like a crescent. Normal blood cells are round, soft, and disk-shaped. The disease is caused by an abnormal type of **hemoglobin** (HEE-muh-gloh-bin). This important protein found in red blood cells carries oxygen.

To develop the actual disease, a person must inherit two mutated genes. This means one from each parent. People who carry just one abnormal gene are said to have a sickle cell trait. These people do not have any symptoms of the disease. But they may pass on the mutated gene to their children.

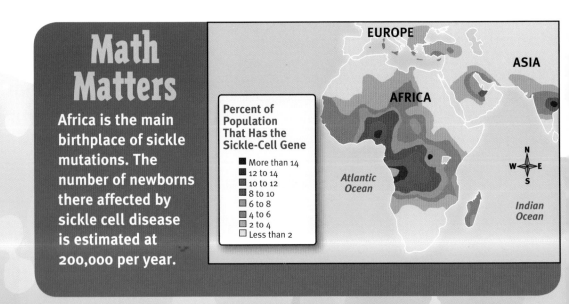

Math Matters

Africa is the main birthplace of sickle mutations. The number of newborns there affected by sickle cell disease is estimated at 200,000 per year.

Percent of Population That Has the Sickle-Cell Gene

- More than 14
- 12 to 14
- 10 to 12
- 8 to 10
- 6 to 8
- 4 to 6
- 2 to 4
- Less than 2

EUROPE
ASIA
AFRICA
Atlantic Ocean
Indian Ocean

N
W E
S

Sickle cell anemia is a painful and life-threatening disease. The crescent-shaped red blood cells have difficulty passing through blood vessels. This leads to frequent blood clots. Clots can damage the body's organs. People with sickle cell anemia need frequent medical treatment.

▼ The round blood cells are normal, while the sickle-shaped red blood cells cause sickle cell anemia.

Historical Perspective

Sickle cell anemia is a serious and deadly disease. However, scientists believe that the genetic mutation that causes sickle cell may once have helped people in Africa survive malaria. Malaria is a disease carried by infected mosquitoes. When infected mosquitoes bite someone, parasites enter the body and attack red blood cells.

Researchers discovered that people in Africa who carried sickle cell hemoglobin were more likely to survive malaria than those with normal hemoglobin. Medical experts are still not sure how the sickle cell trait helps people beat malaria.

Cystic Fibrosis

Cystic fibrosis (SIS-tik fy-BROH-sis) (CF) most often affects white Americans. About 30,000 people in the United States suffer from CF. More than 3,400 Canadians have it, too. The disease is caused by an abnormal gene on chromosome seven.

Scientists have found 1,000 mutations of this gene. The kind of mutation affects how serious the disease becomes. The gene causes the body to produce very thick, sticky mucus. The thick mucus clogs lungs and digestive organs.

People of northern European descent are at a higher risk for the disease. About twelve million Americans carry the mutated gene for CF. One in every twenty-five Canadians carries the mutated gene.

CF is passed to a child by both parents. If both parents have the defective gene, there is a one in four chance that their child will have cystic fibrosis.

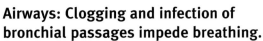

Cystic fibrosis disrupts the functions of several organs.

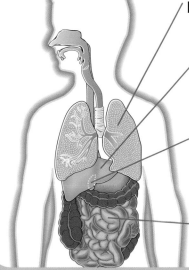

Airways: Clogging and infection of bronchial passages impede breathing.

Liver: Plugging of small bile ducts impede digestion and disrupts liver function.

Pancreas: Blocked ducts prevent the pancreas from delivering critical digestive enzymes to the bowel. Diabetes can develop.

Small Intestine: Blockage of gut can require surgery in newborn infants.

In the past, many people with cystic fibrosis died young. People with CF have a hard time breathing or digesting food. They are also at high risk for infections and other medical problems. New treatments have allowed many people with CF to live longer lives. Today, half of all Americans with CF live to be thirty or older.

Breathing therapy is important for cystic fibrosis patients. ▼

It's a Fact

Tay-Sachs disease affects mostly Jewish people of Eastern European descent. It causes a fatty buildup in the brain's tissues and nerves. This causes children to lose their mental and physical abilities. Most people with the disease die by age four.

Thalassemia (thah-luh-SEE-mee-uh) is a type of anemia. It is most common among people of Mediterranean and Asian descent. About sixteen percent of people with the disease are Greek. So, the disease got its name from thalassa. This is the Greek word for the sea. People with this disorder have abnormally small red blood cells. They must have regular blood transfusions to survive.

Most genetic disorders have several causes. In fact, genes and factors in the environment act together to cause most diseases. Cleft lip and some types of cancer are caused when the environment interferes with genes.

About one out of every 1,000 infants has a cleft lip. This opening in the lip may extend all the way to the nose. The child might also have a cleft **palate** (PA-lut). This is a split in the roof of the mouth. Doctors are not sure what exactly causes the **birth defect**. They think gene mutations play a role. They combine with certain drugs, viruses, cigarette smoking, or lack of vitamins to cause the abnormal gap to open.

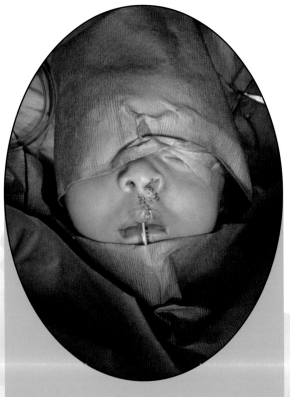

Cleft palates can often be corrected with surgery.

Researchers have found that many different conditions may have a genetic link.

- Alcoholism

- Cancer (certain types, including breast, ovarian, and lung cancer)

- Obesity

- Alzheimer's disease

- High blood pressure

- Depression

Most often, people have surgery to correct the condition. This usually happens while they're still infants. Most people grow up to live normal lives after a successful surgery. For example, Tom Brokaw and Jesse Jackson were both born with clefts. If left untreated, however, the cleft will cause problems eating, speaking, and hearing.

Another mysterious disease is cancer. It is one of the leading causes of death in the United States and Canada. Scientists aren't sure what exactly causes cancer. In the past, people thought the cause was the environment. For example, they thought cigarette smoking caused lung cancer. But the environment alone didn't explain the fact that some cancers seem to run in families.

It's a Fact

Today, scientists are finding that genes can affect the growth of certain cancers. The Cancer Genome Anatomy Project began in 1997. It has created the first index of genes expressed in human cancers.

▲ Environmental factors can cause genetic mutations that result in birth defects.

Treating and Preventing Genetic Disorders

Most genetic disorders are not curable, but scientists search for better ways to treat them. Doctors have many tools to use against genetic disorders. Most common are blood infusions or medicines. For example, people suffering from hemophilia receive injections to help their blood clot. Scientists are also looking for medicines to help patients manage sickle cell anemia.

Gene Therapy

Doctors are trying to treat and even cure some disorders with gene therapy. Gene therapy is the adding or deleting of genes to cure genetic diseases. The procedure is still a risky one. Only seriously ill people can receive this treatment. Doctors hope that gene therapy might one day cure genetic disorders.

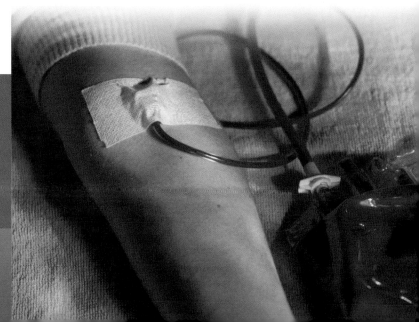

Regular blood ▶ transfusions replace defective blood cells with normal cells from blood donors.

Right now, scientists are doing clinical trials with gene therapy. Clinical trials ensure that gene therapy is safe and that it works well. Scientists study how to best do the procedure. They must also find out the effect gene therapy has on different conditions. If the trials are a success, gene therapy might help more patients with genetic disorders.

Doctors have had several positive clinical trials of gene therapy. Most promising is its use to treat Severe Combined Immunodeficiency Disease, or SCID. SCID is a serious genetic disorder. It causes a child to be born without white blood cells. White blood cells help the body fight infection. Right now, doctors use bone marrow transplants to treat this disease. Bone marrow is the soft matter inside bones. It produces white blood cells. In the future, gene therapy may be used more often.

They Made a Difference

Americans knew little about SCID until they learned about David Vetter. Vetter was born in 1971. He spent nearly his entire life inside a plastic bubble. The bubble was a clean environment. It protected him from viruses that could kill him. His family and friends couldn't go inside. In 1984, doctors tried a bone marrow transplant. At this time, such operations were very risky. A few months after the procedure, David became very ill. His parents took him out of his bubble. He spent his final days surrounded by those who loved him. His situation raised public interest in finding treatments for SCID patients.

Some people are at risk of passing on a serious genetic disorder. How do they know this? Maybe a family member had a birth defect or other genetic disease. If this is the case, a person may choose to have genetic testing. These special tests can help people learn more about their future health. The tests can help them decide if they should have children.

Tests can determine whether a baby has a genetic disorder. New methods of surgery can correct some conditions. This can be done while the baby is still in the womb. Other disorders may result from dangerous body chemistry. Mothers can take medicines to give birth to a healthy baby.

Most women have blood tests and ultrasounds to make sure their baby is growing properly. Some women may undergo **amniocentesis** (am-nee-oh-sen-TEE-sis). During this procedure, doctors take a sample of the mother's amniotic fluid.

▼ Ultrasound images can help doctors identify problems before an infant is born.

☑ POINT

Visualize
Imagine you're a parent from long ago whose child has a genetic disorder. How would you feel if you could see the opportunities people have today for treatment and prevention? What would you say to the scientists and doctors who have made these discoveries?

Amniotic fluid is a liquid that surrounds and protects the unborn baby. Doctors can test the fluid for genetic disorders. About ninety-five percent of all babies are born healthy.

Sometimes the test is positive for a genetic disorder. Then, the doctors tell parents about the genetic disease. The parents learn how to take care of any special needs the baby may have.

For certain conditions, doctors can perform surgery. They can operate on a baby's heart and lungs before the baby is born. They can also give transfusions if the baby has a blood disorder.

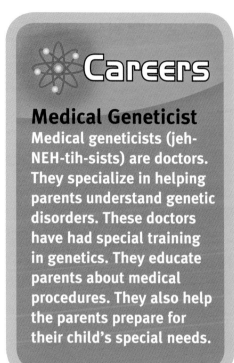

Careers

Medical Geneticist

Medical geneticists (jeh-NEH-tih-sists) are doctors. They specialize in helping parents understand genetic disorders. These doctors have had special training in genetics. They educate parents about medical procedures. They also help the parents prepare for their child's special needs.

▼ Health professionals called genetic counselors are specially trained to counsel parents about genetic disorders.

25

Genetic Engineering

Some scientists want to use genetic engineering to create disease-free humans. Genetic engineering is the altering of genes. It is done to choose which traits a person will or will not have. It could include creating exact copies of a person's tissues, organs, and other body parts. These "cloned" body parts could be used if a person developed a serious illness. Many people, however, are against this. They don't believe in creating new humans or "perfecting" unborn humans.

Everyday Science

In the late 1990s, scientists began combining the DNA of two different animals. This created a brand-new creature. For example, researchers put human cells in laboratory mice. They created pigs and sheep that have human organs and tissues. These new, cloned creatures are nicknamed chimeras (ky-MEER-uz). A chimera was a mythical Greek monster. It had the head of a lion, the body of a goat, and the tail of a snake. Some scientists believe that chimeras can teach us more about how the human body functions, but other scientists disagree.

▲ The chimera was a mythical beast that combined the parts of several animals.

For now, the genetic engineering of humans is still in the future. Today, doctors continue to experiment. They try to find other ways to help people who suffer from genetic disorders.

Scientists are learning more about gene mutations and their exact locations on chromosomes. This may one day help them know if a patient will develop such disorders as cancer. With a complete gene map, a person's faulty DNA can be compared with normal DNA. This would help scientists find faulty genes. Then, they could choose the best possible treatments for any problems.

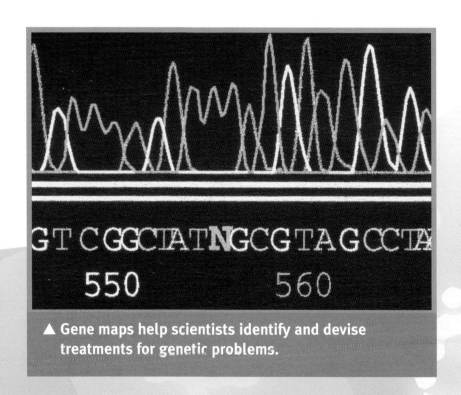

▲ Gene maps help scientists identify and devise treatments for genetic problems.

Conclusion

Genetic disorders are diseases or conditions caused by defective genes. Some gene mutations are passed from parent to child. Other gene mutations are caused by environmental factors. Most people have at least one faulty gene. However, not all gene mutations cause medical problems.

Some genetic disorders are minor. Others are quite serious. Some are even deadly. Genetic disorders are present at birth, but some do not cause problems until later in life. Others may worsen over time.

Long ago, people blamed genetic conditions on curses and other superstitions. Beginning in the late 1800s, however, scientists made great advances. They began to understand genetic disorders and their causes. Today, medical experts are learning more about genes. They have discovered factors in the environment that cause health problems.

A healthy lifestyle can minimize the risk of developing environmentally caused health problems. ▶

Gene mapping has helped the people studying genetic disorders. Scientists mapped the genes located on the forty-six human chromosomes. This information may help medical experts treat or even cure genetic disorders. Despite recent breakthroughs in genetics, there is still much to be learned.

Scientists now know that different types of gene mutations cause genetic disorders. Down syndrome, for example, is caused by an abnormality in the body's chromosomes. Mutated genes passed from parent to child cause disorders like hemophilia.

Many medical conditions have more than one cause. Mutated genes interacting with the environment cause most genetic disorders. Cleft lip and certain types of cancer are examples of conditions with more than one cause.

New forms of treatment can help people with genetically caused cancer. ▼

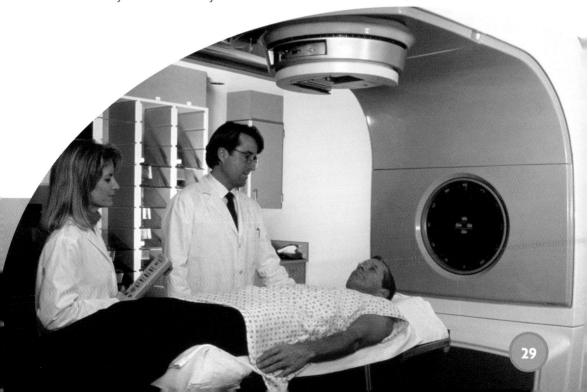

Not all genetic disorders can be treated. Others are helped by medicines, gene therapy, or blood transfusions.

In the future, scientists may be able to read people's DNA. Perhaps scientists could tell them what diseases they may develop. If this were possible, would you want to know? Until then, you can try to control genetic risk factors by keeping fit and eating healthful foods.

Genetic Disorders

Some genetic conditions are more common than others. The chart shows how often new cases of some disorders are diagnosed.

Cystic fibrosis	1 in 3,500 births
Diabetes, type I	1 in 7,000 children
Down syndrome	1 in 800 infants
Hemophilia A	1 in 7,500 male infants
Marfan syndrome	1 in 10,000 people*
Multiple sclerosis	1 in 1,000 people
Sickle cell anemia	1 in 500 African American infants
Tay-Sachs disease	1 in 4,000 Jewish people of Eastern European descent
Turner syndrome	1 in 2,000 to 5,000

*About 30 percent of all new Marfan cases have no family history of the disease.